Desiderium

(Longing)

Wil Michael Wrenn

Wil Michael Wrenn
Desiderium (Longing)

Wil Michael Wrenn
2336 Tallaha Road
Tillatoba, MS 38961 USA

CelticPoet@gmx.com

Published by Prolific Pulse Press LLC
Published in Raleigh, North Carolina USA
May 2024

ISBN 978-1-962374-20-0 Paperback
ISBN 978-1-962374-21-7 E-book

Library of Congress Control Number: 2024905555

Table of Contents

Dedication

I dedicate the following poems

– some old and some new –

to all those who are longing

for something or someone.

Acknowledgments

I express my appreciation to the following publications for being the first to publish these poems:

"Paradox," "Rain," in *Literary Yard*

"Mystery," in *The Pangolin Review*

"I Have to Write," in *Five Willows Poetry*

"Water," "Light," in *Scarlet Leaf Review*

"Paramour", in *Soft Cartel*

"Silence," "House," "Ice Man," "Old Farmhouse," in *Teach. Write.*

"I'll Remember You" in *The Poet Magazine -- Friends & Friendship Anthology*

'Stray,*"* in *Fireflies' Light*

"Hope Is Like a Bird" in *The Pangolin Review*

"Melancholy Days" is taken from the author's second book of poems, *Seasons of a Sojourner*, published by Silver Bow Publishing.

Wil Michael Wrenn
Desiderium (Longing)

"Desiderium" Dictionary Definition:

A longing or ardent desire as for something once possessed and now missed; pain or regret on account of loss or absence.

Wil Michael Wrenn
Desiderium (Longing)

Wil Michael Wrenn
Desiderium (Longing)

Old Farmhouse

I can still hear those voices

echoing from the past,

down the corridors of time –

voices of children

as they run and play

on the long front porch

of the old farmhouse,

warm breeze blowing in

and down across the porch

in the daytime,

sunlight glistening off the tin roof,

white clouds and blue sky above.

Then, at night,

in the cool air and dark stillness,

the voices of the grown-ups

sitting on the porch swing

blend with the laughter of the children

as they chase the moths that gather

and dart at the front porch lights,

drawn mysteriously,

as we all are,

to the light.

Now, nothing is left of those times;

the innocence has faded away,

and the old ones are long since gone,

just like that old farmhouse

that remains as it once was

only in my memory.

The Unsought Companion

Sure, you left;

you're still gone,

but don't feel sad for me –

I'm not alone

for loneliness always was

and still is my constant companion.

I knew it long before I knew you,

but it was never any consolation,

nor is it now.

Nothing has changed…

except time and life,

and you,

and me.

I Have to Write

I have to write...
fragments of thoughts,
embers of feelings join together,
flare up and overwhelm, overflow...

I have to write
to release the pain,
the sadness of brokenness –
broken hearts and souls,
broken hopes and dreams,
broken wings.

Oh, who will save me
from this endless loss
and fill me up with joy,
complete in love

so I'll never, ever
again have to write
unless I write of beauty,
mended hearts and souls,
hopes and dreams,
and healing wings.

Wil Michael Wrenn
Desiderium (Longing)

Hope is Like a Bird

Hope is like a bird;

it will come and go,

and sometimes it will even

make a nest in your heart.

But it will eventually

leave that nest,

take to the wing,

and fly away to come no more,

and you will be left alone

with no one to know

and no one to care.

Hope will have flown

and left only a feather

to remind you

of what might have been.

Wil Michael Wrenn
Desiderium (Longing)

Trees

Majestic, awe-inspiring,

branches reaching outward

and upward

like arms to embrace the world.

Quiet, stately sentinels

watching over the land.

Protectors, nurturers,

even as they are nourished

by the earth.

They give us air to breathe,

and cool us with their shade,

but how often we hurry

to cut them down

to make way for our trivialities.

When they are gone and no more,

they cannot come back again.

We should honor the trees,

protect them, and save them,

for where there are no trees

the earth is less, life is less.

Let us bless and keep them

and leave them as a legacy

for our young.

Remember When

When you are old,

remember when —

when you were young,

and the days were young,

full of promise,

full of hope

and green, growing things.

Remember when

your dreams were young,

and life lay before you

like an open road,

full of endless possibilities.

Remember when

you found love,

and it was right;

you were young,

and you shone like a bright

sunny morning.

Wil Michael Wrenn
Desiderium (Longing)

Remember when —

when you are old,

the days are old,

and the nights are long,

dark and cold,

and the fields

once so green and growing

at dawn of day

now lie mellow in the twilight,

mellow and gold,

soft and serene.

Remember when —

when you were young,

and keep that scene

etched in your memory

like an old portrait

cherished and true,

and when the winter winds

are howling outside,

and the trees are naked bare,

remember when —

when it was spring;

you were young,

and all was green;

love had come

and not departed.

Remember when,

and let the memories

sustain your soul,

keep you warm

when winter comes

and cold winds blow –

remember when.

Wil Michael Wrenn
Desiderium (Longing)

House

The house stands

silent and alone,

empty of the family sounds

that once echoed there...

Nothing remains.

The house stands

forsaken, forlorn,

cold in the moonlight

as the wind speaks

and no one answers.

The house stands

in the shadows,

cold, silent, and empty –

a monument to Trust.

Silence

How can I define a loss

that goes too deep

for words to reach?

How can I describe a loss

that has taken each one

I love so much

so far away from me?

Nothing can fill the void.

No voice can call

from an emptied room;

no tears can flow

from an emptied heart.

To such a loss as this,

to such a loneliness and emptiness,

to such a deep and lasting sorrow,

the only response I can hear

is silence –

silence for an ending

that will never end.

Ice Man

To touch
but not be touched
except inside
where no one can see,
wanting to get close
from a distance,
shy of being seen
and known...

Wanting to touch
and be touched,
wanting to love
and be loved,
but afraid that knowing
means not loving...

So, the Ice Man reaches out,
touches from a distance,
loves from a distance,
and remains alone
in the cold.

Retrograde

I am here.
I sometimes feel
like a non-entity, like I don't exist,
shouldn't exist, don't matter.

I sometimes wish
I had never been born.

Now that I'm here, I don't want to die, but
I sometimes wish, I too often wish I could return
to the time before I was.

I think it must be better not to know anything,
not to hurt, not to be.
I think I would prefer non-existence to
disillusion and disappointment.
I think if I'd had the choice, or had any say
in the situation, any voice at all,
I would have chosen not to come here,
or even exist in the first place.

I believe

suspended animation might be better

than the state I'm in right now.

I believe

I would prefer nothingness

to grief, pain, and loss.

I want to live, to really live,

but not like this,

not like I am now.

I want to live

but not with all this sorrow

and all this emptiness.

It's not even death-in-life,

just this slowly dying

every day, every lonely day.

Here I am.

Gone

Parents gone,

job gone,

love gone,

purpose gone.

What is the point

of going on?

Outer Space to Earth

Above,

the dark cosmos

filled with stars,

moons, and planets,

galaxies and beyond –

a vast, unpopulated emptiness.

Below,

beings of all kinds

reproducing, being born,

eating, sleeping,

living and dying...

and the cycle continues.

Two worlds divided by space:

one filled with life

and one not,

one vaguely aware

and one not --

of what it all means.

Wil Michael Wrenn
Desiderium (Longing)

Free as a Child

I want to drive up to Enid Lake,

walk down to the beach,

take my shoes off,

and run in the sand,

then go over to the levee

and run down its banks

through the grass barefooted

just like I did as a child.

I want to live with the spontaneity,

joy, and exuberance I had

when I was a child.

I want to live free

and full of life and hope,

eager to welcome and see

each new day as it comes,

longing to live as fully as I can

before the night falls

and darkness overtakes me.

Wil Michael Wrenn
Desiderium (Longing)

I want to run barefooted

with the wind in my face,

braced against the ticking time,

holding off its passing

for as long as I can,

living free and joyously,

passionately aware of every moment

until the end comes.

I'll Remember You

You touched me, moved me,

changed me forever,

simply by being who you are.

Please remember me;

I'll surely remember you.

Every time I see a baby smile,

or a Christmas tree,

or falling snow,

I'll remember you.

Every time I hear

the laughter of a child,

I'll remember you.

Every time I see an autumn sky,

I'll remember your eyes.

Every time I hear

the wind whisper softly

in the evening mist,

I'll remember your voice.

24

I'll remember you

every time I see something beautiful,

gentle and good,

honest and true.

Please remember me

because I'll surely remember you --

always.

Stray

I saw a stray dog

trotting back and forth,

up and down,

by the side of the highway,

sniffing the ground,

frantically searching for food.

I had a loaf of bread

in my truck;

I pulled over, stopped,

and emptied it on the ground –

I did what I could.

Wil Michael Wrenn
Desiderium (Longing)

Paramour

He had not loved

or been loved in years;

he had forgotten how it felt.

And then one day

she appeared,

and when he saw her,

in an instant he knew.

Now she comes to him

whenever he needs her.

On moonlit nights they meet

and walk hand-in-hand

over rocky ridge and sandy shore.

On bright, clear days,

they stroll at sunset

along abandoned beaches.

Wil Michael Wrenn
Desiderium (Longing)

On cold, rain-soaked evenings,

they sit by a fireplace

and talk of dreams and wonders.

So, he is no longer unloved,

no more sad and alone,

no longer empty and unknown.

They laugh together

and cry together,

sing and sigh together,

and all he has to do

to be with her

is to call her name,

and she will come to him,

right there by his side.

Then the past with all its

sadness and emptiness

will melt away into the mist

as he leaves it all behind

and starts each day anew,

filled with the presence

of his paramour,

ever faithful, ever true,

his loving paramour –

of the mind.

Wil Michael Wrenn
Desiderium (Longing)

Rain

Days melt into nights.
It's been raining so long,
so long
since I've felt the warmth
of the sun.

Rain taking joy from the day;
rain turning gold into gray;
rain taking all you hold dear
and washing it away.

Days melt into nights.
Love dies on the vine –
not from lack of rain
but from too much rain,
drowning life at the root,
spirit broken, bled to death,
anger spoken, choking breath,
dying embers, what is left?

Wil Michael Wrenn
Desiderium (Longing)

Will love survive;

can love survive

all this rain?

Wil Michael Wrenn
Desiderium (Longing)

Water

I tossed a stone into the water
and watched the ripple it created,
and so I tossed another and then another,
and the ripples expanded...

Suddenly, I fell into the water;
the water rose, first to my knees,
then to my waist, and finally over my head.

I felt myself going under,
and there was seemingly nothing
I could do about it.

I was intrigued by the water
and drawn to the water
because I had been thirsty
for so long,
but now I'm drowning,
about to go under

for the final time –
a high price to pay
for wanting and needing

Wil Michael Wrenn
Desiderium (Longing)

water to nourish me,

water to fill me up,

water to wash over me,

wash my past away,

water to renew me,

water alive for me,

with me, and in me,

but I am swept away

out to sea,

stranded,

with no one but me

to see my folly.

Light

Someone glimpses your soul
because you let them in,

but once you open that door,
you stand naked in the light,

and it's over then.

When someone can only see you
dimly or in silhouette,

half-hidden in partial light,
you are somewhat safe,

protected by the shadows
dark and shielding,

but you reach out
toward a bright and warming light
you vaguely remember
seeing before or seeking.

Wil Michael Wrenn
Desiderium (Longing)

You are drawn to the light;

yielding, you gravitate toward it

because light is life,

and you've lived too long

in darkness.

But you are afraid

that the light will know you,

that the light will see

who you are...

and turn away.

Absence

Sometimes I think I hear

your footsteps, but I turn,

and you're not there.

Sometimes I think I hear

your voice calling out,

but then I wake from my dream.

Sometimes I think I hear

your laughter, but it's only

the sound that silence makes.

Sometimes I think I hear

you whispering softly to me,

but it's only the echo of the wind.

Sometimes I seem to feel

your presence here with me,

but all that's really left

is just a pensive memory...

a haunting, poignant memory.

Wil Michael Wrenn
Desiderium (Longing)

Wil Michael Wrenn
Desiderium (Longing)

The Price

To get close is to get hurt;

that's the way it has always been

with me,

but to stay at a distance,

not let myself feel

or get close, or love,

is not to live –

is to stop living.

But I would just like to be loved

the way I can love,

and to have it last;

I know that pain and grief

surely come with such love,

but, oh, to have loved that way,

to have been loved that way,

and to have it last

would be worth it all.

Wil Michael Wrenn
Desiderium (Longing)

It would bring color, warmth, feeling

to an otherwise colorless, cold,

and unfeeling world –

the outer world

and the world inside of me –

and two hearts, two souls

joined as one, together as one,

never to be parted

not even by death,

would fill up to overflowing

an empty cup, an empty heart.

So, though the price to be paid

for such a love would be pain,

loss, and grief,

I would gladly pay such a price

for without such a love,

life is almost unbearable

and hardly worth living at all.

One More Time

It's strange how you can go on

for so long

without that special one in your life,

and you almost,

almost,

get used to the loneliness

because it seems so much

a part of you.

So you carry on,

or seem to,

and you try to be busy;

you try to be brave,

even though you get so bored

and so tired of it all.

But soon you settle,

or so you think,

into an everyday existence;

then you get lulled

into a false sense of security,

and you're even fooled into thinking

that you have achieved

a certain kind of peace,

and you seem not to notice

the uneasiness all around

and inside you.

Or you push it to the back of your mind,

and all the while you struggle on,

having deceived yourself,

for sanity's sake,

into believing you can make it by yourself

if you have to,

and you're thinking you may just have to.

Then suddenly your fragile little world

comes crashing down

when you meet someone,

and you come upon the emptiness

of your heart,

and you're shocked at the size

of the empty space,

of the gaping hole appearing there.

Wil Michael Wrenn
Desiderium (Longing)

But you feel a faint spark of hope,

even though you've given

so much of yourself so many times,

only to have your dreams

dashed to pieces --

so much so that

you wonder if you have

anything left to give,

and you wonder

if you dare believe and hope again,

if you dare risk it all

one more time.

But you're suddenly made aware

of what you've been missing,

of how false the peace was

that you thought you had,

and so you offer up your heart

one more time

and place it on the altar of life,

a wiling sacrifice for truth and reality,

a willing sacrifice for love.

And, so,

one more time

you give it all you've got

because you don't know how

to give anything less than your all,

and you hope you won't fall

one more time

into the fiery ashes

of a hopeless love,

torn apart, shattered,

burned to death, scattered.

And you pray with all your might

that this time it will be different,

and that, for all your giving,

you'll get more in return

than just one more song

and one more poem

because you would gladly give up

every poem and song

you've ever written,

to have long and lasting love.

So, you say all your prayers

and step out in faith,

hoping your heart is strong

because you feel you can't survive

yet another break;

so, you go for broke,

and you risk your life

for what you need

and trust that the other

will feel the same

and do the same.

Yes, you give it one more shot

and hope this time

love hits the mark,

and when the smoke clears,

that special one

will still be standing with you

with a love that's tried and true,

forever – the two of you.

And with this prayer,

this hope, and this dream,

you lay it on the line,

and you risk your all —

one more time.

Someone

I want to matter to someone,

not just a little bit

but a lot.

I want to be cherished by someone,

to be loved intensely by someone.

Is there any point in living

if you don't mean that to someone?

So, maybe I'm selfish,

but I want to be

the most important person

in the world to someone.

I want to be terribly missed,

grieved over when I'm gone,

irreplaceable to someone.

Wil Michael Wrenn
Desiderium (Longing)

I simply want to be loved

and cherished and remembered,

to leave a gaping hole

in the heart of someone

when I am no longer here.

And while I am here,

I want to be loved

with a deep, abiding love

every hour of every day

for the rest of my life

by someone.

Melancholy Days

Melancholy days,

wrapped in Autumn's bluish mist,

fill my mind

with fading fires of youth;

they linger,

though I would not have them stay.

Wil Michael Wrenn
Desiderium (Longing)

Paradox

Sometimes
I feel I could reach out
and embrace life
and squeeze it to death.

Sometimes
I love life so much
the passion of it
hurts deep inside,
and the more I love it
the sharper the pain I feel,
and the more I sense
the sheer joy of living
the more hopeless and sad
living seems to be.

Sometimes
while flying
I just want to let go
and fall into the water,
sink down to nothingness,
and leave this happy-sad world
of joy, pain, and sorrow

Wil Michael Wrenn
Desiderium (Longing)

to enter into eternal rest

and peace,

but the more I want to leave,

the more I want to stay,

and though death is the way

of escape,

I long to live

and to love

just one more day.

A Conclusion

Who and what I am
and what this life is
I have yet to discover;
the meaning of it all
I have yet to uncover.

The days roll by;
the hours slip away,
but answers elude me
in every way.

Why does God –
Whoever God is –
not reveal Who He is
more completely and more often

but instead
leaves us to guess
and wonder Who He is,
or if He is?

Wil Michael Wrenn
Desiderium (Longing)

Why do hopes and feelings come

that often lead to nowhere

as if in a dream,

a dream that can never be real?

And what are our dreams

but vain imaginings,

ten story buildings

built on sand,

sand that will wash away

when the rains come –

and they will come;

they will surely come.

Our lives, our hopes,

our feelings, our dreams

are like feathers

blown by the wind,

like smoke that rises

into the sky

and vanishes.

Wil Michael Wrenn
Desiderium (Longing)

So, I wonder if I,

if we, if anything

ever really mattered at all.

But one thing I truly believe –

if beliefs have any meaning –

either everyone in this world matters,

and everything matters,

or nothing does.

What Comes After

I long to know

who I am, what I am,

and what I am doing here.

I could have easily died

in my mother's womb —

so she told me —

so, why was I spared?

I long to know what comes after this.

I want to know

by first-hand knowledge,

by tangible, experiential evidence,

kind of like the Apostle Thomas.

Being told about what comes after

by others is not enough for me.

Besides, what if they are wrong?

I want to be told and experience directly

what comes after,

and then I want to tell others.

That's what I would like to do

with the rest of my life.

I have asked the Creator

to grant me this request, but He has not –

He has not told me or shown me.

No matter how earnestly or fervently

I have asked,

The Creator has remained silent.

I still so very much yearn to know,

by personal experience and knowledge,

directly from the Creator, what comes after this

and to be able to tell others.

I have asked, sought,

and knocked on the door for years,

but the door has remained closed,

and the Creator has not answered ...yet.

Still, I continue my quest to know

what comes after.

Dream Flight

I fly a lot in my dreams;

I've often wondered why –

maybe to escape my daytime schemes.

Flying is easy, it seems;

no sky is too high

to fly to in my dreams.

Desiderium (Longing)

Longing for something

or someone lost, or never had –

that seems to be

an almost constant state

of this our mortal existence.

We long for what we had

and lost,

or for what is yet unattained.

Seldom satisfied

with what we've got,

we look to the past or future

and long for what is not.

We mourn over

our failed and faded dreams;

we sorrow over

lost and shattered hope.

Wil Michael Wrenn
Desiderium (Longing)

We yearn for a time
that is no more.

We grieve over those
whom we see no more.

We wait and plod on,
believing and hoping that someday
all that we've lost or yet to gain
will be completely restored
or fully and finally attained.

Meanwhile,
we wake up every day
and go to sleep every night ...
longing.

Wil Michael Wrenn
Desiderium (Longing)

Mystery

I wonder why every living being
must suffer and die.

If I knew the reason,
I would not be a mere mortal man
dressed in these burial clothes,
longing for an answer.

Wil Michael Wrenn
Desiderium (Longing)

About the Author

Wil Michael Wrenn was born in Charleston, MS, USA. He has traveled across the United States and resided in several places, but he currently lives in the hills of eastern Tallahatchie County near Charleston which he considers home. He has a special feeling for the hills, hollows, and landscape of North Mississippi. He is especially fond of Enid Lake, which he considers to be one of the most beautiful, tranquil places he has ever seen. It has inspired many poems.

He has been writing since the age of twelve, first writing poems and then later lyrics and music. He bought a Sears guitar at age fifteen and taught himself how to play.

Since then he has written hundreds of poems and songs and had poems published in national and international anthologies and in magazines. He has also published four books of original poetry:

Songs of Solitude, Seasons of a Sojourner, and *Enid Lake Mosaic,* the latter two books were published by Silver Bow Publishing, of British Columbia, Canada. His most recent book, *Fog,* was published in 2023.

Wil Michael is a songwriter-member and publisher-member of the American Society of Composers, Authors, and Publishers (ASCAP), a national performing rights organization for songwriters and publishers. His music publishing company is called *Autumn Fields Publications.* His website is: *https://michaelwrenn.webstarts.com/*

When not writing, playing music, singing, or teaching, he enjoys family and friends, reading good books, movies, travel, listening to good music, sports, spirituality, and just being out in nature.

Other Books by Wil Michael Wrenn

Songs of Solitude

Seasons of a Sojourner

Enid Lake Mosaic

Fog

Prolific Pulsations anthology

Prolific Pulse Press Author Page

Wil Michael Wrenn
Desiderium (Longing)

Milton Keynes UK
Ingram Content Group UK Ltd.
UKHW021507210424
441441UK00007B/39